Civil Twilight

Books by Margot Schilpp

The World's Last Night
Laws of My Nature
Civil Twilight

Civil Twilight

poems by

Margot Schilpp

Carnegie Mellon University Press
Pittsburgh 2012

Acknowledgments

Thanks to the editors of the following journals where poems in this book first appeared:

Alaska Quarterly Review, The American Poetry Review, Bateau, Boston Review, Cerise Press, The Cincinnati Review, Connotation Press, Copper Nickel, Crab Orchard Review, DIAGRAM, Emprise Review, failbetter, The Journal, Locus Point, Margie, The National Poetry Review, Poetry Southeast, POOL, Snake Nation Review, Sweet, Tar River Poetry, Valparaiso Poetry Review

Book design by Daniel Patrick Kane

10 9 8 7 6 5 4 3 2 1

Contents

IV

I

Civil Twilight

I'll admit it: I have never read Proust,
nor *Moby Dick*, nor most of the Bible,
even though madeleines and Ahab,
Sarah, Joseph, the Epistles, and the Ark
have made their way into my consciousness
by other means, which were necessary,
you see, because I am starting to suspect
that I will never read those books,
and I will never be an architect.
I will never understand whining
or trigonometry, and I will never know
where my first doll disappeared to
in the Landeckers' house. I know
I will never come to love golf.
The load-bearing structures have
already formed in my brain: Crane holds
up, and Eliot. Bogan. The color blue.
An attraction to cotton. A fondness
for the underdog and the addicted.
There is no room for mutton or stiff-
collared men, no place for Splenda.
I want what I want, which is what is.
That's all. No need to argue with me.

Help

Meanwhile I called to the background
help and help and keep me from
falling into the head-basket or

the heart-bag or from crashing
my ribs into the granite with all
its cold shoulders. Too soon the fore-

ground swallowed up the gnaw,
the knives of a lost idea cutting
into the scene and editing

the treatment of the wound.
In time, in time with the stopped clock,
we age. I wanted to defy the figure

and lean of rock and hard,
but places conspire and lips
call No, no, if you want to try

again, that's up to you, but here
we are all out of help and eggs
and every other damned thing.

On Not Making Arrangements

Organization is overrated: rivers
show us this.

They also decline telemarketers' calls
and aren't bothered

by prayer or phobias, which I believe
precludes them

from much but to look pretty
so that paintings

can be made. Scholars write about
the influence

of Huntington's Chorea on the slant
of the brush

or the exact moment when form
became the dorky

kid brother of function. In the oxbow,
answers collect

like algae. Perhaps there's another
kind of peace

to seek, and water can take you there.
The estuary disrobes

at low tide. You may vanish
in the sarcasm

of fluids one day. From your apartment
above the local pub,

you watch the bodies enter the rooms below.
They're aimless,

accidental. If you believe that orchestration
or planning

can take the place of beauty, perhaps
the joke's on you.

Confessions of a Nanotechnologist

The teensiest of the tiny technological spurts
winks its little eye tonight: too soon for mass
production, but too late to cure the leukemia patient

who just expired in room 1407, bed B, even
amid laughter and smoke that fogs the visionary
outlook into an ordinary form. There are the usual

bedsheets to change and fluids to empty
into receptacles marked with biohazard symbols,
while the family retards the flame of grief

until they are immolated in their own living
room. Take heart that the vision is clear
in at least one mind: the smaller the better,

and make it snappy. The molecules rest
in their colloids. They Jekyll and Hyde:
copper becomes transparent, solids become

liquids at room temperature, gold turns
catalyst. Let it start something, then,
and let the properties be altered, within

reason, for structures need something
to count on in the crazy micro-world.
We don't like spoiled children,

and we don't like rules that can't be broken
into a million atoms exercising their right
to assembly. They won't be arrested, won't

be standing by their nanocars with flat
fullerenes. It's every atom for herself:
they drive me nuts with their ambitions

and their fears, the cocktails they drink
for courage. Yes, anything's possible,
including fuel catalysts and sunscreen,

but I like the idea—urging in its infinitesimal
voice—being suspended in the colloid
that transforms present to past, future

to present. We may not even know when
we have it in our hands, but
the old truism is, after all, true: size matters.

Wow

The real collector doesn't know what he wants.
—California sculptor Bruce Beasley

Someone thought mutated vegetables
in the shapes of shark penises or a perfect human ear
should be labeled and set on this shelf

under the antique Russian executioner's sword.
Someone donned the curator's coat
long enough to fall

victim to hoaxes or purchase a medieval ape mandible
for more than the price of a suburban home
at the peak of the bubble. There has to be a way

to make people say *wow, that's amazing*—
to wonder at the sheer doggedness of a single collector
who'd spend years amassing all the known tools

humans have ever used to groom their eyebrows.
When I was a kid, I remember marveling
at what seem now like ordinary things. Friends

of my parents owned a Renoir. They reserved
an entire wall for the painting,
though it was a tiny rectangle washed

in too much light, and for years, too short,
I could see only the frame's margin.
Bruce Beasley, you are my hero,

with your fine assembly
of skulls, but I also have been astounded
by things just taking up space in the world, by random

placement and accidental beauty. Maybe
our fascination with what we thought of as real
is at an end, and we're peeking

into the opening of a new exhibit.
My brother collects and collects,
but says he's going to thin

by half. Half of the chairs go. Then half
the china, half the milk glass, half the flatware.
Half the plants in the garden? Half the cement cherubs

or Lladro figurines? Half the grand piano?
Can he relinquish the feeling of having
enough that all these objects provide?

One vacation in 1968 found us wandering
across Europe, through mazes of objects: glassed-in,
framed, standing in corners, suspended

from ceilings, mounted on little platforms
and lit by subtle, correct light. See
what we have rescued from the pit

of history? Still, I am grateful
for also being fascinated
by the idea of the things, rather than always

by the things themselves, for finding wonder in
the phenomenon of the cabinets
that hold the timepieces and salt dips

and relics and arrange them all
into idea and memory. That summer
we took it all in. We drove

halfway across the Continent.
We stopped at museums and castles
and every made thing on all our maps.

Subliminal Brain Track #47: Automobiles

Here it is, already dusk, and the cleaners
will be closing, probably before I get there,
which figures, as does this man pulling out
in front of me in his silver Lexus.
He must not have kids if he drives like that—
though that's probably good, for them

and the rest of us somewhere down the line.
My dad taught me to drive in a '76 Dodge Dart,
dark green with a brougham top and a slant six
that's probably still running these thirty years on.
He took me down to Campus Lake, let me
navigate the hairpin turns by the water,
his body a little rigid in the passenger seat,

a little like how I would be years later
when I snuck him out to drive one last time
at 93 in my mother's gray Accord,
around those same curves that bordered
the water. The State declared levels
of PCBs too high to safely swim,

but driving by was another thing,
though brown swirls of muck foamed over
the shores and most of the plants had died.
And I used to drive around the lake a few times
to sober up, have the last smoke of the evening.
Smoke didn't tell me anything in San Diego.
There, it was chugging, then stopping.

At the side of the road, I changed the fuel pump
in a '79 Mercury Capri bought used
from my Midwestern high school's Prom Queen.
My small hands—greasy and nicked—fit
into the cramped spaces, even holding the wrench,
as a friend read to me from the Chilton

repair manual. Tighten this. Loosen that.
Turn counterclockwise. Remove adhesive paper.
Once, my parents picked me up from day camp
in a new used Olds 98. It was
a kind of powdery green and had power
everything, including power brakes
that went out at a stoplight two days

after we brought the car home, so my dad eased
into oncoming traffic honking a dead horn,
then bashed into the yellow traffic pole
in classic slow-motion, while cars swerved
and slowed, and steam rose from our hood.
Steam became a leitmotif. Or was it smoke?

So hard to tell from a distance or
in the side-view mirror, where objects
may be closer than they appear: what's behind
is in the way if you're in reverse, the people
you love getting restless in their seats
as the scenery does what you don't expect.
Better get out of its way.

Gravity

It's a force to remember on those nights
you imbibe too much at your local pub—down
you go, Guv, and up you come with the rug's

bold pattern splashed across your damp face.
Pretty. There've been a lot of falls.
There've been that same number of risings.

Getting up is simply remembering to work
against gravity. Once you're in the clouds
it's a different story: flight

reckons the sum of air and allowing someone
else to be in charge. You saw the lilies growing
in the garden, the taxi idling at the curb,

and everyone was serious.
Now, the moods are harder to gauge—
for the falls, we can rise and shake off the dust.

For the rest of our lives, we'll understand gravity.
No one falls under the spell of tartan or brocade,
or sees the cheeks' faint flush rise like tiny suns.

Once in a jacket of sunlight
I walked the horseshoe path of the park.
I was looking for a dog, or a bucket of carnations.

I found grass and a path cutting through weeds.
The clouds lost me in superlatives. The sky's maze
went nowhere I could maneuver, and in the store

window a doll's dark eyes assessed passersby.
No one sees the vacuous expression of the clerk.
It redeems us, this pantomime: hold

your hands up to the imagined mirror and push.
That's the limit of your power.
The flat wall that stops you.

Décolletage

Say it: a robber in the neighborhood
has stolen your conscience. A train
makes its way, steel and tarry ties.
The trestle rumbles under a barren sky.
It is daybreak in the moonshine.
The still burps satisfaction and soldiers
have abandoned their regiments.

Come home to find courage.
Every day is antebellum somewhere.
There's a noose swinging, windsock
horror and mama curls her child's
neck against her thigh.
Say it: these ghosts may not rise
against the bars of our chests.

Good Girl

Sometimes I neglect to wash my hands
or lock the door, but I'm a good girl.
My grasp of the world

is dismal. I use words
I don't mean all the time, saying
candy when I mean pain,

breast when I meant to say weapon.
But that was how I came to things—
idiosyncratic, the mind changed:

one minute a pink frock, bending
back for a kiss, and the next
still in my pajamas at noon,

foaming toxic froth
at my husband. That's not the way
I'd organize the world. Not by half.

II

Iowa Sonata with Combine and Squirrel

I sit in the back row of the Baptist Church
and watch my older daughter blend herself
into the group of kids here for the first day
of Vacation Bible School.

They shuffle, gaze at the floor,
then introduce themselves. They spell
out J-E-S-U-S. They clap and make universes
with their arms. At first it sounded

like she was saying Bobble School.
I pictured little apostles, saints
and sinners, the paired animals from the Ark,
everyone with big wobbly heads.

I believed in little at her age: grass,
sky, that no one would like me. I believed
that time was inexhaustible, thought the world
was a place I would come to know.

That summer, one piece of tinfoil
was enough to wrap the television's antenna
and grab the one good station
coming from Chicago. I had a ball

of a radio, one that kept rolling
out of my bed. I had a phone that stood up
and looked like sculpture. I thought I was sophisticated,
but I was already a consumer.

Everyone's faith has been loaded
smartly into these rifles to walk around, guns
cocked. It's too late to prevent the bells
          from ringing. Their strange peals

          sail through the air, deep and mean
in the evening. I love the kisses of web
and wiper, the slash of keys and grille
          against the fast lane's wind.

          Outside, a squirrel stands on its hind legs
to get a better look into the bucket.
All the simple things complete themselves,
          and on the rim, a bit of salt.

          Time is an inelegant trick to turn us
into different people. It is summer.
It rains. I tighten the sharp,
          red tourniquet of love.

                    *

If the laughing starts, I'll know something's wrong.
The gum I picked up on my shoe? That someone's
snipped a hank of hair from behind me? Some fool

     could blow us off the planet on a whim, and I know some
     of those men and women who've become derailed.
     The train blew through town and forgot to blow its whistle.

How long will it take to walk downtown not looking behind
after each few steps? How many days or hours before
     the ringing of bullets slows down in their ears?

In the evenings there are noises that I can't identify:
　　skritches and churrs and hiccuppy curls of breath. This new world
breathes, even when we're asleep and even when the cats bathe

or the birds gather discarded string for their new nests.
After sundown we turn off the air, then open windows.
　　It's quiet so that the suction noise sounds loud. Bats emerge

　　from behind the shutters. They enter the winds like wind—
　　　　more a feeling they're there than seeing them fly by.
　　It's that quick, the way time suddenly shows you your irrelevance.

You have children, so they're your relevance. Then they're
your replacements. Other people's children will marry yours,
　　and you'll live, then die. Before that you can notice

　　the certain way the orange marigolds are planted around a tree,
　　　　or how each streetlight's been donated and has its own little plaque.
　　You could mark the rooster motif carried out

in the local diner's decor, the "quitting a bad habit,"
"fresh start/divorce" and "infertility issues" specialty cards
at the local Hallmark store—cards for all occasions.

　　The farm equipment store sells more grills and chainsaws
　　　　and hedge trimmers than combines and troughs
　　and hay racks. For years in my hometown,

　　there was an empty building on the way out
of town. It would open as one thing then shutter
itself again. It was like walking backwards:

no one could see the path he was on until it ended.
But there was such a variety of failures: Sav-Mart.
A liquor store. A pharmacy. Mohr-Value. A Rural King.

The crashing of many visions into one reality: location
matters, and a small town in the depressed Midwest
isn't really any location at all.

*

The leaves quiver and shimmer in our humid air,
as the jet
              trails and power
                            lines bisect
the sky. I am waiting for legitimacy to claim me,

but for now, it's all a sham: this cup
of coffee,
              this highway sign,
                            this muddle of plastic
and beef and cotton. In the sand, I see

what look like ears, curled shapes emerging, to hear
the sad sunlight
              sizzle into
                            the moon's skirts. Under,
quickly, I find shade and a cool, cool expanse

of calm. It's time to move the chifferobe, to
close drawers
              and hang up
                            the towels left
on summer's floor. Take a deep breath: your sky

and mine are the same. I wish there were cottonmouths
circling the plumage
     of the shore,
          but all that's
there is a small sparrow, an expanse of cement

baking in the sun. At the cafe, there are
imitations of Miró,
     art popped then
          multiplied, like flashbulbs.
That light conspires to bleach out, to melt, to

blanch. It won't be fire or ice: this highway's
mud, this slag-
     heap town's left
          behind a door
of cool iron that never says a last good-bye.

*

He rolled a cigarette and stuck it into the side
of his mouth, then snuck out the back door to find his car in the lot.
There were a lot of nice ones out there. What camaraderie

exists at the mercy of surplus. When the trees lose their leaves,
you bet. When the price of gas falls below four dollars
a gallon, you bet. When can one notice the final cut

in the price of oranges or bread? One day, the lines appear,
and the next, the registers are empty, along with the drive-in theaters
and campgrounds. It's as cheap to stay in a cheap motel.

Forget baths and miniature golf. Your vacation
could consist of therapeutic breathing and high colonics.
There are occasional bumps in the road, thumps

from upstairs, where the karate school just opened.
I watched the sun bend down to meet the horizon, heard
some grown men moan about where the big turkey plant is now.

They don't remember the future, can't fathom how
the kid's haircuts and baggy shorts will turn to business casual
and spit-up-stained shoulders. Time does tell. And moves us

to the margins, then beyond. In more than one window
I saw some holes drilled. They were letting people drop
business cards into the gaps. The stores are still inside.

The key is conversation: you must ask for the account
of how your grandmother pretended not to be married
so that she could still work at the phone company.

You have to divine from talk that she noted the guests
and gifts at birthday parties for her four children every year
until they left home. There won't be a spare root cellar

holding boxes of family history: you're responsible to seek
it out. One tone rings out of the air conditioner, a brisk hum
that cools the room and your desire to go anywhere but here.

Too hot, the day that's arrived, and too light, the sunshine
sending down its reckoning. I love the certain way
the fern's shadow wavers on the library's carpet.

The tenor seeping up from the quiet room. The life here
is a new kind of old-fashioned: connected, simple, aware
of itself in the lightness of the summer, the cool fall airs.

*

In the diner, the men refer to each other by which tractor
    he drives: an International, a John Deere 2010 or 2020.
They discuss modifications made and crops to come.
    In the background, the news, but it's from far away:
Boston, Washington, DC, Japan and the G8 Summit.
    This is not the 4020's going back to Canada
and this is not the accident that happened last night
    up the road a piece. The lakes overspill their boundaries
and land in my backyard. I see the shenanigans
    of the trees and walk through imagery not of my making.
A squirrel on a chair eats from an ear of corn.
    The world turns into itself, again; my vision
has always been the same. See what's in front of you
    and imagine the rest. Extrapolate the broader vision—
and you'll be fine. What if the presentation clock
    from the Class of 1913 tips over and lands
in a glass heap at my feet? What if the wands
    my daughter begs for from Target
really are magic and can disappear the world?

*

The world is a dangerous place for these generations and we know it:
let us play in traffic and go extreme. We deserve a little fun

before the last moments of our dying world light up the sky
with the coming of the end's scream. Eliot said a whimper,

and maybe that's where we'll end, but right now, we scream.
We're holding out our arms, embracing the bang

before that whimper. It's nice to think of how patterns repeat:
one moment, the next. Your chest rises into the morning's light.

Think back not to divine, but to *worship*: the return of each return.
When I saw the river's bottom, I saw the old sky turn

into the next world's firmament. The sky lets us open our eyes
and see the lid of death. One open moment and the creak

of birdsong fills the pit. If fire can extinguish the world,
let's light the fuse and set it now: a warm glowing end of the day

that seats twelve. Turn to your right and look at what's next to you—
a girl? a net? a pail of dust? Allow yourself some murmur

of happy greetings before the music ends and you're alone
again in the corner of your room. Time is still a graceless trick

to remind us of impermanence. In this room a cat has found
the barley growing on the windowsill. Outside, the squirrel stands

on its hind legs to get a better look into the bucket. All
the simple things complete themselves and, on the rim, another bit of salt.

III

Optimum Conditions

Out the back, the riverbed
        a deep flow of hair, a nest,
a break in phrase and dance.
           Find the crack and mend it.
Flax, feather,
       an idea
              shimmering
under cobalt and violin,
              the circle of straw.
The egret stands on one leg,
walks nowhere. Flight
       is merely some late geometry
practiced too soon. Silt
       fills the grooves, then fills
the memory
           of grooves.
                If this were music:
up-tempo, cheer
       and boundless waves
choreographed into arc,
into plume and beak.
       If this were hue:
chartreuse glinting
       under yellow, the sun's
twin dressed better.
       I keep a veil
           and sand
under the kitchen sink.
           I keep trying on
other lives and finding

no fit. There used to be
citrus groves for miles, constellations
            of lemons, galaxies
of oranges
                        sweetening
under the sun.
            An aqua convertible
                        lurches through
the scene on its way
to Havana,
            on its way to Miami,
            suicide doors and fins,
an imagined song drifting
            from its radio.
                        Down-beat,
upswing, a torchy standard
            silkening the mood
into cool
                        or almost like
            love's bones
humming.
            The shore, the canal,
a violent storm washing
            in shells that don't belong.
It's a travesty and a miracle—
                        you see the chips
and grinding
            from a quarter mile away.
Sweet-tempered money
            spent too fast,
                        and it's all
washing into a tide-pool:
            shell,

pocketknife, a camera
             broken from its strap.
Vacations and in the strangest ways,
but after folks go home
             there's still salt here,
enough to preserve
             a way of life from passing.
The sun stutters,
             behind a cloud.
      The light changes,
then changes again.
The bird's balance wavers
      but she steadies herself
and returns
      to poking her beak into the water,
looking
      for the reward she knows
she'll find
      just below the surface,
             given the undertow,
patience, and the wind.

Rediscovering Fire

I'm not your carousel horse,
fierce teeth turning
to nip a thigh.

I'm not a pincushion
by grandma's chair, not
the bark of a familiar tree,

not a trail you could follow
in the dark. Maybe
I'm a snowstorm in summer,

a map emerging
from the earth, bearer
of a new legend.

There was a wedge
and a hammer splitting
time. Old keys opened

new doors: papyrus,
telescope, virgin. If oranges
are left on a sill,

they darken and rot.
What does it matter
if clerks across the country

call me donor?
The wood crackles, hot
and bright, a tiny storm

in a column of light.
Random burning happens
in our houses and our hearts.

Let Them Watch

The middle of the night found me on the road
to Aranjuez. I was going to find the garden
and make it bite back its regrets,
but it made the aviators buzz the cornfields

and the clouds be blown to the corners of the canvas.
The magma moved away from the core
because ultimately heat is a repellent.
You can walk on igneous rock all the way.

And you can find the drone in the sky,
with its dark engine, falling thousands of feet.
And you can find an elevator
with its buttons already lit, a stop at every floor.

Recall will kick in when you use what you learn:
speak a foreign language or find your way
to town in a dozen different ways.
Be suspicious of a life that looks too good,

and be suspicious of anthropologists.
They'll kiss your lids
then put you in a study. Let them watch
through the parent-proof glass: all the moves

they're being taught will work later
when they're wheedling the car keys.
Let them keep lists of the types of horses
that thrive in deserts, or the protocols

to follow when reporting a suspicious death.
Let the alter egos shine: there's guilt
and shame enough to feed them for years.
Sometimes the only master of a trick

is the person who's never performed it,
but that's not you. You have experience
with everything from drawing cartoons
to making risotto. Everything is as real

as everything else: pita bread and sweat socks
and baskets and the parts of speech.
Make sure you watch, and remember,
everything your eyes claim
out of the opaque whisper of the screen.

Score

In the meantime, I sang. I tuned myself
            to the pitch of dreams. I sang.
                        I sang about species
                                    and habits, and the feel
of hammers, about war
            and emptiness. A lot

of the time, I trembled
out of tune,
    or hummed, waiting
    for another voice
            to propel me forward. My mother sang to me,

rocked my cradle painted
                        the color of dandelions. Space
        filled itself
                up. I meant to drown
                out static
                        and confusion. I meant to persist
                and reckon.
        Songs were populated by dragons
                        and daisies,
                                    by cries
        for help, by heroes sung.

My hands stilled.
                In the meantime,
                        the songs replayed
                themselves without voice and without sound,
            in my head's radio

blaring inward. The words
               were subliminally absent, like a train
backing into itself
                    and disappearing. What was left
          was the absence of each note, each step
                    on the scale's ladder untrod.
So I backed out on command, took
               my clef
               and staff,
                    took my voice—
not singing—
     into the sea.
                         The feeling of camaraderie
abandoned me. I abandoned
               the delicate machinery
     of surprise.

In the meantime, I waited.

I tuned myself to the pitch
          of silence.

Everyone waited for words to be unsaid.

Everyone
          worried that
                    what might be said
          would be like our dreams:
                    shadow, sorrow, loss,
     the undersides of joy.

In my bones
        lemons ruled. In my bones a forest
            of longing
                        was contained like a century, contained
like driftwood
            possesses gray. And there was
                        a need to be rapid, to snake
    my fingers into the dirt

            where earthworms heard
                    music distilled
by clay and regeneration. Half of a body
                    and half of a body
            joined together
            in a dark charade
of forgiveness or beauty, or the echo
            of the sound
                        all my music made,
        its graceful, gorgeous
            melancholy shawl
        trapped in the gyre
                        of the throat
I couldn't remember how to use.

Cumulus

In fact this hyacinth squatted on all the space
in the garden, left a tattoo of purple bleeding

into the air, where a palm-shaped cloud slapped

a print across the sky: No Vacancy. You check in
anyway, delicate and clean. You borrow the light

*

from the streetlamp to read about a crime.
The end comes like a curtain on fire, intense

heat disappearing into the conversation you had

years ago with your mother's college roommate.
You argued about beauty, whether it is altered

*

by light and luck more than cosmetics or grief,
and about whose kids were more successful.

When the fire flashed up, all appetite, afterglow,

there was no more to say, no epiphany
about that night, no sweet apology to the dark

*

forces, no do-over or rat's nest or canine teeth
filed down to mimic politeness. The shift

was complete, the phoenix flew into the clouds

and mingled with a hippo and a chair.
You sit to think and nothing comes close

*

to the way your mind went around and through
Shakespeare and Donne, parsing the flatnesses

speckled with words that turned fugitive, turned

rust, and the clouds keep shifting. They alter
themselves. They look—briefly—so solid.

End of Summer Dithyramb

                    That's a lot of wine you've got there,
          but I can help
you drink it, and we can smash the bottles
          into the rocks
each time we finish one, then watch
          the sparkly shards
                    wink up from the crags. I'm sorry
I didn't wear
          that great red dress because red is pizza
and apples
                    and blood and sexy fingernails hovering
over the skin
          on a stranger's back, even if his yacht
is moored
                    at the farthest end of the quay
and walking
          to it in heels endangers. Red is also
the Canadian flag
                    pouting on a windless evening. Let's dance
to Canada,
          to old friends, to new friends, to wine
and the lips
                    to drink it with. Let's drink to dancing,
          to friends, to living
from one suitcase for a whole summer,
                    to never and always,
and, for good measure, to sometimes.
          The harbor lights
stray across the eye each time we spin,
                    and sadnesses

drop away like gulls leaving the sky.

       Let's have more wine,

              more dancing, more pure stars passing

their light

       into history's sky. The boat rocks against

its ropes;

       the ropes strain against the tides.

          Summer's tail

       is disappearing around August's last leg,

so let's set

the life vests afire, toss them behind

          the boat

into the water's deep appetites,

       and let's learn

each other's names so that someday

       we can tell this story

right down to that, with the glittering

       shards that catch

          the reds of the sunset and of the wine.

Advice in the Form of Confusions

I have been watching the young
struggle through their daily lives
and waste the flesh we all remember
and I have seen the gardens they shine
their leaves in, the kind invented
by distraction and devices that run
on little lithium ion batteries, flat
disks that power music and voice
into strong tremble and staccato chain
that barrels into the angelic orders
we raise our heads to see, or hope
to see, but never do, for they have
sprung into louder volumes and faster
rhythms that disorient and confuse.
There are sounds we can no longer
hear, at our age, and we don't want
anymore to know what we left
behind on that sill or under
that abbreviated sun. I can't know
wry substitutions. I can't hear breath
embrace five-minutes-ago or tomorrow
and there must be a word for that,
but I don't know it. I know the sound
of thinking a hard whistle into the lung.
I know the shape of houndstooth
and the hang of each tag's pricing
itself out of so many's reach.
I swoon and recoil at the tresses blowing
in an arbor without glow
or flame. These are reprieves. Respites

in the demands of sensation
and flow. Know this: you can you can
you can you can you can.

Secrets

They emerge, surprise and storm, into the light
they blink under. See the attempts
to stuff them under the couch cushion
or the rug, to wrestle them to the floor. Help
them emerge into the treaty of civility—
no fussing around the neighbor's wife, no revealing
the location of the treasure. Pick the lock
that conceals marrow and rhinestone, the stuff
of fantasy that subsumes
Sunday dinners with family and the nitty-gritty

fill-the-car-with-gas necessity driving
us into the poles. There is no sense
asking to take yourself off the list. There's no chance
to restore your good name. I can't tell you
how many bundles of bills are lodged
in your fireplace or whether daffy Aunt Minna
meant to leave that beautiful castle of stone
to her favorite cat. I can't even tell you
that the future is worth getting to.
Some of the bright stars twinkle into nonsense,

but I know they're not nudging me.
I know the small miracles of every clean basket
of laundry and the origin of not telling.
But not telling holds the whole of history
hostage to the possibility of light. Two little
girls try to sell lemonade and cookies,
but their futures depend on a hundred million
people, all of whom have things not to tell.

Hear that silence loudly and know: the blessing of a secret is not in the keeping but in the telling.

Kicking Digger Out

Into the night's dampness go the Milk-Bones,
the dented silver bowl, the faux-sheepskin dog bed.
They knock up against each other, then land

next to the chain-link. Digger slinks
toward the far fence, his head bobbing low.
Yes, throw out the dog, then deny

you need help. All the thinking you can do
is done with a knife at your throat.
But when the swallows come back

to Capistrano, something changes in the air.
The clerks in the little cafés, the boutiques,
and the souvenir shops smile and ask

if there's anything else. There is:
limos beached on hills, unable to move
because they're too long to get over a hump.

And: Mary Todd Lincoln selling manure
to pay off the local department stores.
Things may not change, but maybe they become

more amusing when viewed at a distance.
I can't settle this bet: who wins
when everyone is lost? I have tried taking

each side and the other. I have wept
and rent my clothing. The dog is still
not allowed inside. He has made friends

with the collie a couple of yards down,
since the row houses' yards are in a row, too,
and abut each other, a giant quilt sewn

by metal. The dogs yip at each other,
hike their hind ends up in the air
and splay their paws. As it begins to get dark,

the collie's owner calls her in, but Digger stays
and stays. He's an old dog and knows
that when someone tells you *no*, maybe
they are simply talking to themselves.

An Explanation of Women's Undergarments

Flesh gives a tug, spills slow-mo
toward where the ground whispers *Come down*
here. I must meet you. I thought never
never would gravity visit,
for I am not a welcoming host.

No matter. I have friendships
with nylon and spandex, with contraptions
designed to prevent and lift and shift
this skin to that place. The dressing room
is not a friend and this is not vanity,

not exactly. The brain says chocolate
ice cream pasta French fries bread.
The brain says *whoa!* and *wow!* and *never*
an 8 again, but I can't listen since I'm full
of *I am still 24,* and also full of temptation,

which is really a kind of hope
that what I know will happen
won't happen after all. So so so
the gorge and guilt, at least
a little, and the minefield the buffet is:

Crab Rangoon—Bang!
Cornbread—Bang! Fried Chicken—
Bang! Bang! Bang!!! I'm standing
by a lava lamp, by a piggy bank,
by Bleyer's mysterious mannequins

that have no nipples. I'm in another
dressing room, this time with a woman
and her tape measure. I am
mortified to show my breasts-to-be
to this stranger. I flee.

I think shampoo I think a cool
pink and gray plaid skirt I think
a pleated navy dress I think anything
but having to go back and try on
stiff white bras. Olga. Warner.

Playtex. Bali. The names sounded
like vacation spots or friends.
I would have liked to travel from that body
turning into not my own. I would
have loved someone to confide in:

I'm scared everyone will notice me
or *I'm afraid some boy will snap*
the back to hear the sound it makes.
My mother finds me mooning over
the rainbow of Pantene bottles lined up

inside a glass case. They cost $6.50,
more than a month's allowance.
But you don't have to try them on.
No one will cup your almost-breast
in her hand and pronounce a size.

To Dad from Bob, Christmas 1939

—Homo sum humani nihil a me alenum puto.

A simple square adorns the spine,
        identifies this book as *Roget's Thesaurus*
of English Words and Phrases, a gift
        from my step-brother to our father

years before I was born, and used
        so well it was re-bound to keep
its pages from continuing
        to flutter singly, unexpectedly dropping

opposition and *co-operation*
        from the lexicon my father needed,
his second language learned
        on the fly, as needed, after

he emigrated at 16 from Germany.
        This book harmonizes and moderates,
causes and inserts motion
        into the stagnant pool of words.

Think of the cusp of a war,
        powers trying to talk to each other
and diplomacy practicing its hand
        on the stubborn force

caroming out of its national bounds.
        Think of the scarcity of paper,
of the dilemma for the son, the book
        signed *from*, not *love*.

There had been a divorce and a division
        of the contents of the house,
and years when visits were stiff
        dialogues and accusations

that never broke the surface. The words
        are here: *acrimony, provision,*
insufficiency, cruelty, waste, friction,
a family awry. So the gift

must have seemed a gesture meant
        to mend, to open a channel
long silent. But my father was not sentimental:
        He would have used the book

as it was meant to be used,
        may even have quickly forgotten
it had been a gift at all,
        since its value was accrual, aggregation,

clarity and precision, not the trigger
        of a heart-sent hope that more
than single words would pass between
        the father and the son:

their correspondence shows reserve,
        a strain and surface reportage,
not dimensionality extended. Not camaraderie.
        Not intimacy. There would have been

little for my father to pack
        after the divorce: he lost.
A new beginning, then, and that, too,
        is contained: *resume, re-start, commence.*

And diminishing contact, sparser
        each year—news, perhaps,
of a job or a marriage, of a move
        to another town. Maybe there was time

to think of how long it was between
        conversations, but I think it's more likely
that cereal was eaten and mail was opened,
        floors were swept and through

it all the book kept hold of all the words
        that could describe a life: *labor, obsession,*
diligence, loneliness. The book saw far
more of my father's face than Bob did.

Little Black Dress

for my mother

A filet is cooking in the pocked saucepan, steam
rising as steam does,
and I am thinking of sorrow,

which is also like steam—warmth
and permeation, movement to the edges
of a room, to a ceiling where droplets

fall back down to drown you again.
I have known sadness
in the light and dark, deep

keening silent in the heart
though it rearranges my face and seeps
into others as steam and heat.

For the service, I am ironing
a black dress.
Fabric smoothes over the board,

a black waterfall. I am saying
I'm sorry, I didn't mean, I never meant to,
but there is no one here, only

the thickening wind.
There is the hiss
of the iron and the wind.

The untranslatable cord
wraps itself
around the air.

In the closet the dress hangs.
In the closet I witness
its demise: soft neck bending.

In the Key of C

Her name was Edina and her hands
turned sheets of music in the dark,
though her house was always lit up and had an aroma
of powder and fish, as if she'd tried to start dinner
during someone's lesson and forgotten the body
simmering on the stove, jumping a little in the grease,
and then burning a little in the heat, and then,
since fire extinguishers then weren't high
on anyone's list of things to have around the home,
she'd scampered into the bathroom and found a tin
of Jungle Gardenia dusting powder to smother
the growing flames. I went there once a week
for years and, for years, practiced at home a half an hour
every day, which made not a whit of difference
in the quality of my play. In the expectant hush
before recitals, you could hear her panty-hosed thighs
rub together as she walked across the stage
to introduce each of us and what piece we'd play.
Every now and then I'd miss a lesson, but
even blood-poisoning wasn't enough to avoid
having to perform "Flight of the Bumblebee"
in front of a crowd of people all waiting to hear
someone else. I hope the torture of sitting
on the hard bench, back straight, fingers poised
in position, and her metronome pulling me along
as I stumbled and scrambled through each song
I hadn't really learned at all helped my parents
decide eventually that I was wasting my time
and a lot of their money, especially since my brother,
whose hour preceded mine, and whose talent

dwarfed mine, could play almost anything
by ear and after hearing it only once. I sat outside
her pink house and listened to Grieg, to Handel,
to Bach and Beethoven and Mozart, to the Beatles
and the Moody Blues, slither out of the threshold,
and wished for some kind of destruction—tornado?
flood? murder? stroke?—to pre-empt the anguish.
There on the astro-turfed steps, I'd sulk.
The word *wretched* came to mind, and *inept*,
and *misery*, and, eventually, *quitter*.

IV

Charmed

Little statue of Ganesh: you are the Lord
of Obstacles

and Beginnings. Carry me
over the rocks

and burning asphalt to the bright circle
of wisdom.

There are dead insects in reasonable condition,
and if you mount them

properly, you'll hardly see the damage
from the grille.

We'll never all agree, not on everything
and not on this: air

holds nothing but a pledge.
Criticism

is for indoors, for piano teachers and parents,
not for this

broad sunlight and not for love. The secret:
make sure

the injuries don't show. I need a map
and a lot of luck,

so I carry charms and use them. Evil eye,
ward off

the obsequious. If such things are possible
in the confusion

of myth, say nothing. You must unbuild yourself
and reassemble

into a more pleasing shape: a teardrop, a fin,
a trunk, a mole.

Waiting Up

Night is the edge I know,
and when all the insects

disappear, I stitch worry

into the upholstery
of my heart. I've made a blanket

to sleep under: proof

of what exists, a search
for the lost, a hand closing.

I watch the door for buckling,

feel the knob. Its paint shows
images that may be madonnas,

a sextant, or the sudden whip

of desire. I have a point here,
and it's *if*. It's *when*. It's *I think*

of our cells colliding.

After the party, I went home
and sang hymns in the branches

of our tree, my lampshade discarded

and many empty plastic cups trailing
behind me like breadcrumbs.

All these days come and go,

snails and beatitudes.
I've thought of you and the clock

keeps telling me you've gone.

I've wept into my hands and fallen
into a bloody stupor. I've found that

without the compass,

the needle's simply a metal point,
lost in a hive of air.

Concealments

In the future, when daguerreotypes break into inkblots
      that screen for pessimists and crazies, a handful
can tell the future of any river or toy. Flow
          down, burble, flow down. The water assimilates
and shines across the heavy nests of time.
     There will be no tongues by which to injure
or worry, no breed too ridiculous to own.
       This way, the Bowie and butter will mingle
in the fat drawers without license or complaint.
       This way, bandwidth and cursive will speak
the same messages to each and every.
         How long the wait for faith or canticles
to descend into the trees. How aromatic
      the waters of grief: deep down the scent is fear,
and the lights humming keep time keep time
         keep time forever, until the image is captured
as best it can be, which is to say imperfectly
      perfect, the blur and smudge a part of all
the ways we almost see what we never saw before.

Gratitude

Left to my own devices, I'd have burned
out years ago, but there were those who saved me:
Mrs. Treece from second grade, with her argyle sweaters
and hidden clues in spelling tests, with her ability to sway
even the most stubborn toward cursive and the Pledge

of Allegiance, which was not then a joke but an exercise
in remembering the sounds air and music combine to make
in children's mouths. Let's say I was rescued and set down
in the garden of destruction, California, state whose letters
can be rearranged into 132 other words. There, a story

can be told from the perspective of a car or the point
of view of the rat. One listens nonetheless and hears
tales of salvage and ruin. No one remembers to ask
about the spinster aunt or reckon the statistical truth
of theft. Thank you, Candy, for clean needles

when I couldn't be bothered to protect myself.
Your apartment was an oasis of feather boas
and size 13 pumps and your shows
were glittering amalgams, exaggerated homages
to Judy Garland and Barbra Streisand. Whatever

form you inhabit now, I hope your saving me
bought you some good karma in the cosmic tilt-a-whirl
we rode. I am thankful to my college advisor
who offhandedly mentioned that graduate assistants
in English earned fifty dollars more a month

than those in Sociology. I can appreciate
the considered advice as well as the accidental nudge.
So it pays to notice when something goes
missing. Something dies. The denouement contains
a surprise: the goblet of manzanilla set in the first scene

on the mantel. All along it was waiting there.
All along, it was both secret and key. Notice
how the arcs resemble the farcical red arrows
of a company's success, how recovery
depends more than a little on reputation and chance.

On Not Following Instructions

My carnival of fear, my candy pain,
the clambake night going on and on,
while two continents away, embers
buzzed, beautifully glowed long
into the next week of char
and fossil, the details
a little disconnected
and more than a little strange:
see the credit card slips taped
to windows, see the red dress
she wore hanging
in the town square. This is
another country making
an exception
and a ruin
of a natural kinship
gone deeply whole: bravado
can't account for everything,
but in the phrasebooks
you'll find *machismo, macho,
manly*, and *where is the toilet?*
You must cross the paths of geese
and stand still in the desert.
You must surrender
your favorite book to the hand
of an enemy.
You must underline every
other word on every other page,
then relinquish
the dithyramb.

No matter. There's no place
for it now, in your life
where somber music
follows you like a puppy.
Moreover, history will deride you.
Go ahead and slip
on the dress. Run.

Monsters

*We have also seen, that, among democratic nations, the sources of
poetry are grand, but not abundant. They are soon exhausted: and
poets, not finding the elements of the ideal in what is real and true,
abandon them entirely and create monsters.*
—Alexis de Tocqueville, *Democracy in America*

And think: how astonishing, the turns
    the tongue learns before poetry matters at all—
        the proper breath, the coordination

of all the complex things that have
    to happen: conscious thought, the proper
        muscles moving, the easing of our

control—the only thing keeping
    us all from bad behavior—
        some undiscovered force.

You might call this a conscience.
    You might think of it as civility.
        But the neighbors could just as simply eat

us as live next door for forty years.
    There is a hearth in that stone,
        a smoking heart, a body heat angel

in the snow. And still no word
    of the McKinnon's girl who blipped out
        between the roller rink and the family

car. Still no name for the body they found
      that winter on the Piper's farm. Oh, there
            are breakdowns of the mechanical kind:

that barrier keeping us from the worst
      of ourselves grows thin and can't repair.
          We'd think of it as beautiful, but then—

no microscope, no research grant—
      that quickly, the deed.
          Done. Went. Gone.

Coming of Age

How do you package a revolution?
Clean living takes a holiday
along with telephone service,

and a little sentiment is inevitable:
outdoor dancing spreads rapidly.
There is little doubt that who
happened to be toiling had also

fallen out of sync, for industry
informs the aesthetics of an age:
death by car wreck, death by falling

from a great height, death by
pesticide or prayer, boarded-up
houses and decaying stores—
some moral governor has locked up.

A little sentiment is inevitable
when there are things to remember
watching: a little statue

of the Madonna to comfort
and protect as she sails away.
More than anything else, there
is the feeling of being kept

in a cage, of having taken a holiday
to the hangout of a legendary
America: abducted while playing

golf, inheriting someone else's
fortune. At first, conversations
rarely moved. "Destiny destroyed
my life and I don't want to be

told what to do." The desire
to create beautiful art took over,
and the indigo dye used

on the robes suggests an entire
social class. Put all the myths
to rest. Become able to sing
without tears. How do you

package a revolution? Use
the new typography, cause
insomnia, see the others' points

of view, for lush celebrations
have made thousands—in
the most delicious of
tortures—dance.

At Rest in the Throat of Air

Brueghel! And an image springs already formed,
even prematurely framed by gold
acanthus leaves, but

this dark panel by the younger one, by Jan
(also known as Velvet Brueghel),
departs: a covey

of ornithological variety,
captured in fugitive chromatics.
Tenebrous landscape

dotted with lustrous birds, almost a field guide
peculiar to no geography.
Birds balance on limbs,

gather and wait in their motley formations.
And in one of a plump woman's hands
the spindly bouquet

of contour and tail feathers, of filoplume.
She holds her arm like a bastard wing,
a scarlet fabric

draped around her nakedness. Not shy, modest!
Cherubs, too, hover menacingly,
clouding the airscape.

Bare bottoms and chubby thighs almost pedal
to remain aloft. But still the birds,
airborne or earthbound,

are what seize the eyes; they have to keep coming
back to every pinnate spot of paint,
to each and every

bird he brushed: tern, ostrich, peacock, blackbird, owl.
Whooping crane, ringed plover, steppe eagle.
Blue-checked bee-eater.

And this is our inherent vice: one must see
what one thinks is there before one sees
what is truly there.

Great crested grebe and plover . . . a graylag goose . . .
We ignore that tiny chariot.
We don't see horses,

no gold watch, no sword, no armillary sphere.
No gloomy vampire bat escaping
near the tree's faint trunk.

Customs

I have nothing to declare.
There's nothing inside my suitcase
that shouldn't be there.
There are no eggs.
There is no currency.
I do not have any fruit. I am out of cheese
and pudding. There is not an ounce
of meat. I have not secreted a porterhouse.
I gobbled the last of my pills
before I boarded the plane. I couldn't swallow
the balloons of heroin. I am not a mule.
I have nothing to declare.
I travel light.
That is my raincoat.
Those are feminine hygiene products.
That is a hairbrush.
There is nothing else to say.
I have nothing to declare.
You do not need to look in my bags.
There is nothing to find.
I do not have any monkeys.
I do not have any orchids.
There have been no illnesses.
I have nothing to tell you.
I am hoping to come back the day after tomorrow.
These chocolates are for my hostess.
I have nothing to declare.
I will not be bringing back anything unusual.
Please let me through.
I apologize for the lateness of the hour.

There is no reason to search me.
Please, take your time as you riffle through my bag.
I have nothing to tell you.
No one has asked me to carry anything.
I would not do so anyway.
My luggage has been in my control.
These bags are mine, all mine.
Please. Let me through without delay.
I have never made a bomb.
I do not know any terrorists.
I am not an expert at incendiary devices.
I am an expert at language.
I have nothing to declare.

Making a List

I want a way to convince myself
that captains of industry had it wrong,
that greed isn't something
to aspire to while starlings sing dirges
into the fog. I want
not to want anything.
I want the apples never
to brown into mush,
the trees never to need
pruning. I want the dozen
long-stemmed red roses my prom date
didn't bring and a Waterford vase
to put them in. It happens
too often: you wear your bones' cathedral
out, spend a good amount of time
in elevators or libraries and I want
never to know what else
I could want—because it's endless, the list:
gold bullion, yacht, harbor, beachfront
property, music lessons, purebred dog,
stable, football field, gewgaw, trinket,
tchotchke, figure-head, vessel, airplane,
landing strip, six-pack, pretty
child, omelet, toast, train.

Little Hymn to Plastic Surgery

And the stars felt good anyway, even
in the daytime when no one could see them,

even while my attention
was focused on what passes

for stars here on earth, and even
though candlepower is how

we measure light, not star-power—that's how
we measure trauma. Show me falsity,

the superficial shine and spark.
Watch it design the night's gown,

watch the haphazard become the only
way any of this makes sense: down

to the same world, down to the simple
courtesies of calling and excusing.

There was only one more thing to do:
apologize. She did. And it was

poison. The gravel clacked against itself
and spit to the sides of the road.

The places it lands are the places it lands.
One can always shuffle.

Fear waxes everything into place.
C'est bon. The rest of perception

rings the bell. It is here: bow down.
Lower. Bow down.

Grasp

Moreover that would be the gulf
between handiwork and disaster:
a small piece of sunflower hanging

on a thorn when the sun browns
the grass and roughs up our skin.
Some of the last of the meat

hangs across wooden poles,
and it is full of holes. At least
the salt licks and trailheads converge

and the animals roll to spread dust
over their skins. I can only imagine
wanting to relieve an itch so much

I'd nuzzle into the dirt's embrace,
with its beard or tattoo clutching
the skin and letting a dark cape drop

over the rounds of our shoulders.
It could have been condensed milk
or brownies burning in the oven,

or the cusp of hope dissolving into
something more bitter and hard
to swallow. But the rides slowed

and we got off, stepped into the dust
and left footprints trailing into puffs
of cloud, then were gone.

And the ride is over, and the drying meat:
smaller than it was at first, but still
pliable. I could take one down

and bite it, but the grip wouldn't be
the same. Some of my teeth are replicas.
Still, the important move

is the letting go, the opening
of the jaw to let a friend's hand pull
out the meat and not catch
the soft underside of his wrist.

Black River

In every attempt, a success
of sorts: render the whole
of our rivers into visible or into still.
The places I've been are many.
I attended *Dr. Tulp's Anatomy Lesson.*

I rode a horse out of *Guernica's* planes.
Always, it is light or dark
and I hold visions
of resin and pigment and stone,
of steel and light, of gloss

and glass and straw and mud,
optics, and remember that it's all
atoms, this world imposed.
Say I'm looking at a plan
of the Palace of Versailles.

Say I'm willing to walk
its Gardens. The growing.
The dying. The passage of time
into idea, idea into sequence
and back into time, this cacophony

and harmonious melding
of what ascended like the sun,
like a king, like bread
in a peasant's kitchen. If we are
to memorialize, how to do that

now? By visiting the Parthenon?
Taking off my shoes outside
Hagia Sophia? Putting
the Venus of Willendorf
into my back pocket? Or by invocation:

Rodin's *Hand of God*?
Or Brancusi's *Bird in Space*,
a slippery smooth unfeathered thing
balancing the future
against the whole of history

against all of our fetishes and idols,
all the deliberate placements
of paint and sweat on canvas
and ceiling, patterns
that pass down like genes—

egg and dart, papyrus, archway,
column, four-leaf clover pressed
into a favorite book. I mean
to say how I fit into history's
little diorama—I am a mote,

a scale, a bit in an ancient
horse's mouth. In these places
cells gather at the corners
and who's to say they won't
one day be a creature with all

the knowledge we've lost?
You and I still look
like the Demon of Luxury
at the Church of La Madeleine.
You and I often sit in the lower right

corner of Chagall's *Time*
is a River Without Banks,
and we devote some brain cells
to the North Rose Window
at Chartres, its colors fueling

the search for a perfect blue,
a generous green. What's visible
on history's horizon is everything
until now. What's invisible
is everything, too. To see

the future, I rode the spine
of Saarinen's Arch, looked out
over the city, where everything's
so small it matters more. When
it's gone, it will matter most.

In my mind, I saw the roads grown
over, cracked, impassable.
The river was a black snake
of sludge, carrying away
the concept of time,

asymmetrical spires, mortality,
a wishbone of hope:
great monster of cells
that just might rise and
devour the thought

there are miracles.
The beautiful water
became black
snow. We cannot tell our boots
from what they walk in.

Channels

The emergency test noise from the television
      catches in the lit glow and across
the actual knob, over the curved screen,

          and into the chipped veneer on the cabinet.
If only a little snow blinked on, the pierce
      of the alert would alternate with a shush or wheeze

or something to break the note. Outside
          the sun was shrinking down, a red shawl
covering the land's shoulders

      to dark, to cold, to another evening
in the deep winter's crush of smoky air.
          It permeated everything and left itself

for dead. The crawl ticks by again
      and if this were a true emergency
we'd have another kind of panic, though how

          the silhouette of fear could muscle its way
farther into our psyches, or how
      the windows of our permanent flight

could close and lock themselves
          on waterboarding and hoods, we can't be sure.
There is space to apologize to the days

and each turn of the ancient television's dial
brings us back to the mid-20th century
        with its halitosis and endearing use

of iceboxes and fins. We can run no more
        from worms and snakes, from polluted
memories of weird nostalgias.

        The entryway's flowers are wilted
and dropping their petals into a little mound.
        In another month, we'll hear the noise again,

unless we awaken from stupor and design.
        Could we try on our mothers' feather boas,
our fathers' smoking jackets, and teeter

        around our living rooms in borrowed
grownup shoes? The most we can give
        is the most we can give and still it is never

enough. Deeper pockets. Wider eyes.
        Stamps in our passports defy the shrinking
of our worlds. You can pack your jello

        and tea and dryer sheets and nicknames
into one small suitcase to accompany you
        to a dream and a scourge, the torn dress

there's no thread to mend, the carpet
        with a permanent stain.
Don't fall for a stranger's twisted tale

of the Fata Morgana. Don't settle for a partial
eclipse. It's all or absolutely nothing,
        in the end, and in the end breath and

the remnants of breath are all we have to heat
    and speak and move the equations
of fair play and mercy

        into the fast lane, onto all the channels,
through the quiet air, boundless, full
    of promise, and free.

In Retrograde

The wind is music
in a great cathedral. I can not

pray here:
I taste apples,

hear hollow chords.
When a book

is closed, the pages go dark.
Gravity rises

up this body,
and the fragile kite

of beauty
is already flying away.

Some previous titles in the Carnegie Mellon Poetry Series

2009
Divine Margins, Peter Cooley
Cultural Studies, Kevin A. González
Dear Apocalypse, K. A. Hays
Warhol-o-rama, Peter Oresick
Cave of the Yellow Volkswagen, Maureen Seaton
Group Portrait from Hell, David Schloss
Birdwatching in Wartime, Jeffrey Thomson

2008
The Grace of Necessity, Samuel Green
After West, James Harms
Anticipate the Coming Reservoir, John Hoppenthaler
Convertible Night, Flurry of Stones, Dzvinia Orlowsky
Parable Hunter, Ricardo Pau-Llosa
The Book of Sleep, Eleanor Stanford

2007
Trick Pear, Suzanne Cleary
So I Will Till the Ground, Gregory Djanikian
Black Threads, Jeff Friedman
Drift and Pulse, Kathleen Halme
The Playhouse Near Dark, Elizabeth Holmes
On the Vanishing of Large Creatures, Susan Hutton
One Season Behind, Sarah Rosenblatt
Indeed I Was Pleased with the World, Mary Ruefle
The Situation, John Skoyles

2006
Burn the Field, Amy Beeder
The Sadness of Others, Hayan Charara
A Grammar to Waking, Nancy Eimers
Dog Star Delicatessen: New and Selected Poems 1979–2006, Mekeel McBride

2002

Keeping Time, Suzanne Cleary
Astronaut, Brian Henry
What it Wasn't, Laura Kasischke
Slow Risen Among the Smoke Trees, Elizabeth Kirschner
The Finger Bone, Kevin Prufer
Among the Musk Ox People, Mary Ruefle
The Late World, Arthur Smith

2001

Day Moon, Jon Anderson
The Origin of Green, T. Alan Broughton
Lovers in the Used World, Gillian Conoley
Quarters, James Harms
Mastodon, 80% Complete, Jonathan Johnson
The Deepest Part of the River, Mekeel McBride
Earthly, Michael McFee
Ten Thousand Good Mornings, James Reiss
The World's Last Night, Margot Schilpp
Sex Lives of the Poor and Obscure, David Schloss
Glacier Wine, Maura Stanton
Voyages in English, Dara Wier